# CYBER WITHIN

*The Security Awareness Story*
*(and guide)*
*For Employees*

D1314453

## Marcos Christodonte II
MBA, CISSP

FIRST EDITION    JANUARY 2010

For additional information visit our website at:
www.CyberWithin.com

Cyber Within/ Marcos Christodonte II -- 1st ed.
ISBN-10: 0615330150
ISBN-13: 9780615330150

Editor: Ann Guidry
Developmental Editor: Eric Parizo
Cover Design: Cathi Stevenson
Cover credit: ©iStockphoto.com/jsemeniuk

Printed in the United States of America

"Through education and training, users develop an understanding of threats and form an alliance with their organization to thwart them."
                              –Marcos Christodonte II

# CONTENTS

## Part One: The Story

## Part Two: The Lessons

# Part 1

## *The Story*

# Chapter 1

## You're Hired

Roxy, a young college graduate, was eager to make her way in the world. With tens of thousands in student loans to repay and a wedding to finance, she desperately wanted to land a decent-paying job right out of school. Her fiancé kissed her goodbye one beautiful Monday morning and wished her luck on her interview for a data-entry position. As she drove to the interview, she attempted to recall every paper she wrote in school about business and leadership. She thought the interview panel would certainly ask about working in teams, organizational management, and building data models—all subjects she studied in school. She was particularly excited that her first interview was with the YNS Group, which was her top choice as a place to start her new career. Not only was it one of the most well-regarded companies in the area, but it also had a reputation for investing in employee training programs and promoting from within.

As Roxy drove into the parking lot, she took in the dozens of rows of cars lined up in front of the huge mirrored glass building. It seemed to reach right into the sky. She thought about what it would be like to make it through the ranks to a senior-level position with the company. She suddenly felt butterflies in her stomach and began doubting her ability to make a good impression. After she parked her car and started walking toward the building, she happened to kick a small USB thumb drive that had been lying on the steps to the main entrance.

When Roxy picked up the drive, she noticed what appeared to be an engraving that matched the initials of the company's chief technical officer. It read: W.O.Y. for William Oscar Young. She remembered him from a presentation he gave at her university. Roxy was impressed by his speech and even shook his hand afterwards. All of a sudden, Roxy was no longer nervous. She was almost sure that recovering this device would endear her to the interview team. Then Roxy started thinking about all the possible company secrets and sensitive documents she may have saved the YNS Group by keeping the thumb drive from getting into the wrong hands.

After asking the secretary for directions to the interview area, Roxy sat patiently waiting. Instead of practicing her bio or thinking about how she would respond to tough questions, she wondered if the USB thumb drive in her pocket did indeed belong to the CTO. Ten minutes later, a tall, much older man walked up and asked if she was Roxy. The man introduced himself as Doug Barnes, senior director of human resources, and escorted her to the interview room.

As Roxy entered the room, she was taken by surprise. Not only did she see a long mahogany table with crystal, water-filled pitchers and elegant chairs, but sitting in front of her were two department managers and the CTO, William Young, who apparently stepped in briefly to ask one of the managers an important question. Roxy wasn't sure if she should mention the USB thumb drive, and was left speechless as the CTO said hello on his way out of the room. The introductions to the department managers and seeing William were a bit much for Roxy to handle, so she interviewed without mentioning the thumb drive.

The interview went surprisingly well and Roxy was offered the position on the spot. Despite her inexperience, the managers were impressed with Roxy's personality, ambition and knowledge of the company. Roxy accepted without hesitation and asked if she could start as soon as possible. After she and her new supervisor, Ralph, agreed she would start the next day, they went on a tour of the office and signed the initial paperwork. Since the normal in-processing area was being renovated, Roxy was taken to an office near the director's area. Roxy used the internal portal and a temporary password to fill out the new-hire paperwork online. Since most of the forms were electronic, Roxy asked if she could save her copies electronically as opposed to printing hard copies of everything. When Ralph told her this would be fine, Roxy suddenly remembered the USB thumb drive in her pocket. "Rats!" Roxy said to herself. She felt she missed her opportunity to make a great impression on the CTO. She thought if she went back to give it to him now, it might appear inappropriate or out of order since she had not mentioned it earlier. Roxy decided instead to use the thumb drive to download her personnel files. She thought she could take the drive home, save her files, and anonymously mail the drive to William. "Besides," she rationalized to herself, "I already have the job."

Roxy pulled the drive out of her pocket and inserted it into the computer she was using. The computer suddenly became very slow, so slow it seemed the files weren't copying anymore. The cursor froze in one area and the keyboard didn't allow her to use any of the function keys. She waited a few minutes but the computer failed to respond to any commands. She was just about to reboot when she suddenly heard the sound of numerous phones ringing. She quickly realized they were helpdesk phones ringing at the IT support area around the corner. In just a few minutes time it sounded as if the number of calls increased a hundred times. She got up and peeked around the corner. From there, she overheard people in the halls asking if each other's computers were working. It dawned on Roxy that *she* might have damaged the network. The USB thumb drive might have downloaded a virus that may be spreading from computer to computer like wildfire! Just as she turned her head to look back at her monitor, a message slowly scrolled from the top of the screen. It read:

*You and your network are now 0wn3d by Team W.O.Y.*

*Thanks for using our thumb drive and giving us access to your company's trade secrets.*

*Regards,*

*W.O.Y (We Own You!)*

# Chapter 2

## The Fun Begins

Roxy began to panic as she realized what she had done. She dove under the desk and flipped the switch on the surge protector on the floor. The computer in turn went dead. Roxy then snatched the USB thumb drive out of the computer and tossed it in the trash. She considered hiding it in her pocket, but considering it was the digital equivalent of a smoking gun, she didn't want anything further to do with it.

Just then Ralph popped his head in. Since the company's computer systems had been suddenly and mysteriously thrown into chaos, Roxy's new boss told her to leave; processing a new employee could wait, but dealing with the fallout of the computer problems couldn't. As she left the building and drove home, she had time to think about what happened. Roxy felt horrible about the incident, but wondered how it may affect her job. She didn't want to be known as the new employee that brought the network down.

The next morning, Roxy arrived for her first day at her new job. With the USB device still dominating her thoughts, she coyly asked her boss, Ralph, what had happened. He told her the IT department and CTO were very worried. At that point, they were unsure of what caused the systems meltdown. Because they needed time and resources to recover from the computer attack, they predicted it would take several weeks to discover specific details about the incident. Fearing legal action, Roxy thought about the possibility of being blamed for the attack, which had already been estimated to have cost the company $1 million dollars. She considered leaving right then, but realized the company's computer forensics experts could likely track the attack back to the exact computer and time when she was using it. If they traced the intrusion back to her, she thought, they would definitely think she was part of a larger plot. Roxy decided her only option was to figure out how to get rid of the evidence pointing straight at her.

Not wanting to ask questions that could raise eyebrows, Roxy decided to turn to open source information (OSI), otherwise known as publicly available information, to research how she could track down the evidence. She didn't know what to do or how to do it, so she decided to poke around on the Internet to get some ideas. This way, she wouldn't appear to be snooping through company files on her first day. She remembered reading an article about how a former governor and presidential candidate's e-mail account was hacked using OSI. Apparently, the hacker used the email provider's password-challenge questions to reset the account password. The answers to the secret questions, which asked the governor's birth date, her ZIP code, and where she met her husband, were all easily found on the Internet.

Roxy figured if she knew the key players in the IT department and their responsibilities, she might be able to get some useful information that could help her. She thought back on the computer security course she took as an elective to fill out her schedule, and was suddenly grateful. She remembered that computer systems can be very weak, especially if they aren't adequately updated with the latest security fixes. From this, she knew she'd eventually have to access one of these systems. Before doing so, she would first have to find out what kind of security system the company used, then figure out how to access it. Roxy was headed down a dangerous path, and she had her work cut out for her.

Roxy used Google to begin searching for information about the YNS Group. She typed "YNS Group" and "phone roster" and got nothing. She then typed "YNS Group" and "organizational chart" and got nothing again. Then she remembered a way to "hack" Google by using advanced searches to find almost anything. She still had access to online lectures found on her university's website, so she pulled up her notes from one of her computer security classes. This gave Roxy her first "Ah ha!" moment.

Using her notes as a reference, Roxy inputted the following query into Google's search engine: site: www.YNSGroup.com ".PPT" to find anything with a PowerPoint brief. Bingo! She found company briefs, conference agendas, and an organizational chart, among other things. This gave her the name of the IT director and the names and phone numbers of each department manager. This was valuable information she could eventually use.

Roxy decided to see if she could find out which security systems the YNS Group used, hoping she could find some information that might help cover her tracks. At this point, Roxy realized she might be getting in over her head. She said to herself, "I'm just a data-entry employee with a college degree." However, the thought of losing her job and being held responsible for the million-dollar network damage only cemented her resolve. She felt if she could cover her tracks well enough, she would surely escape being blamed.

For a brief moment, she thought back to the long job search she'd just endured and the dozens of applications she had submitted. But then, she realized something. Most companies' job listings include experience requirements for systems they own. This clue made Roxy go back to the YNS Group's site and look under "Career Opportunities." She clicked on the most technical-sounding position that appeared: firewall engineer. That job listing had requirements for an experienced engineer with a background in Cisco's ASA Firewall. The listing read that the firewall engineer is responsible for maintaining all network security devices. These devices monitor and log all network activity, and are critical for troubleshooting, audits and investigations.

She decided to stop her search for now and consider her next move. That night, Roxy could barely sleep. She had read many stories in the news about people breaking into computer systems and couldn't help but think about how she was planning to do the same thing. She just hoped she could avoid making headlines along the way.

# Chapter 3

## The Prowler

Roxy showed up to work and distracted her managers by claiming to have a lot of HR paperwork to finish. She also planned to skip the new-hire orientation meetings she was supposed to attend. Her managers assigned her a temporary cubicle to work in while they looked for a permanent desk for her.

Roxy saw the phone in front of her and decided to pull out the company roster she had googled the day before. Looking at the organizational chart, she saw the name of the Director of Information Technology: Christy Salvador. Suddenly, Roxy decided to think outside the box. She had the thought to impersonate Christy, the director.

Roxy considered calling the service desk and pretending to be Christy. She could try to get the service desk employees to do what she wanted. Without giving it another thought, she picked up the phone and called the service desk.

The service desk answered by saying, "Good morning, Mr. Henry. How can I help you?" Roxy quickly hung up. She hadn't even opened her mouth and they thought she was a Mr. Henry. Roxy was astonished. She balled up her fists, shoved them into her cheeks, and rested her elbows on the desk. After glancing around, she noticed a stack of business cards belonging to Rick Henry. "Of course," she thought to herself. She was sitting in Henry's desk temporarily. Every phone was assigned to a specific employee. Roxy now realized that in order to impersonate the director, she must somehow access her desk.

Roxy went to the break area, down the hall from where she was sitting. She started thinking about how much tougher covering her tracks would be than she originally imagined. As she walked down the hall, she saw the HR manager giving what appeared to be a tour of the company to a new employee. Roxy decided to greet the HR manager, but suddenly slowed down as she approached him. She overheard them discussing how the employee would be responsible for protecting the company's critical network infrastructure as the new network operations lead. This gave Roxy an idea. She stopped at the water cooler and listened closely as the two approaching men talked. She learned the new network operations lead's name was Travis and that he would report to Christy, the IT director. Roxy turned her back to them, attempting to avoid attention as they walked past the water cooler.

Roxy's brain went into overdrive as she stopped to process this new information. She knew she first had to gain access to the IT director's office. She sipped water and pondered a few ideas on her way back to her desk. Roxy decided to do a little homework on Christy, the IT director. This time, Roxy used Bing to look for information.

Roxy typed into Bing, "Christy Salvador" and "YNS Group." Since her name was somewhat uncommon, Roxy got few results related to anyone other than the director. Right away, Roxy noticed Christy wrote various articles for IT magazines, and had a profile on several social networking websites. The first website she noticed was a networking site for professionals. The other, Facebook, was a social networking site for friends and acquaintances.

Since Roxy had a Facebook account, she decided to log in and see how much information she could access. Roxy was able to view Christy's full profile without even requesting access, or in Facebook terms, asking to be her "friend." Roxy started prowling through Christy's personal information. She noticed that Christy was married, but that her husband appeared to be traveling. From what Roxy could gather from some of Christy's posts, he was possibly deployed in the military. Roxy also noticed that Christy sent frequent messages to a younger guy, and that the conversations seemed to be more than friendly. She took note of the guy's name, Todd Daley, and decided to put the wheels in motion.

Roxy called a local florist and requested that a dozen roses be delivered to Christy Salvador after lunch. When asked if she'd like to leave a note, Roxy said, "Absolutely. Please say, 'Christy, we've been chatting a lot lately and I thought today would be a good day to leave work early and meet for dinner at Sal's Italia. Meet me at 5:00 p.m.' Please sign it 'T. Daley.'" Roxy chose Sal's Italia because it was a very private and intimate upscale restaurant located close to the YNS Group.

Roxy remembered the director's area was near the room she was in when she used the USB thumb drive that brought down the network. She walked to the area and looked for Christy's desk. As she got closer, she walked right by the office where all the trouble started. As she continued walking, she saw Christy's office. The door was open and Christy was inside working. Because Roxy didn't want to be seen, she headed over to the break room adjacent to the director's office. She thought she would wait there and make sure the roses arrived.

Roxy sat in the break area for over an hour. She told other employees that she was locked out of her office and was awaiting the key. She was afraid she might tell the wrong person, possibly someone who unlocks offices, so she changed her story after a while and began telling people she was waiting for a colleague. It was almost 4:20 p.m. before the flowers finally arrived.

Roxy got up and peered down the hallway a few times, looking into Christy's office. She saw a big smile on Christy's face, and it looked like she was packing her things and getting ready to leave. As Christy left her office, she closed the door behind her. Roxy went back into the break area and waited a few more minutes. When she was sure Christy had left the area, Roxy walked to Christy's door and grabbed the knob. It was locked. Roxy dropped her shoulders in utter disappointment. At that moment, a man pushing a cleaning cart came up and asked if Roxy was okay. Taken aback a bit, Roxy answered that it had been a rough day. The man asked if she had locked herself out of her office. Roxy, completely surprised, answered that she had and asked if he could help. Since the janitor had a master key to the doors on that floor, he was able to unlock the door for Roxy.

Roxy thanked the janitor, quickly made her way into Christy's office, and shut the door behind her. She noticed all sorts of paperwork filed in piles on the desk. She saw a more up-to-date organizational chart than the one she had been using, a couple of incident reports, and a bunch of printed-out e-mails. She read the e-mail on the top, which was from Christy to her deputy. In the e-mail, Christy appeared to be talking down to her deputy for under budgeting on a project. She threatened to decrease his bonus to make up for it. Immediately, Roxy realized that Christy seemed to be hard on her employees. She decided to use that to her advantage. Before she picked up the phone to call the service desk again, she thought a moment about what she should ask. Then she looked down at the organizational chart. She saw a blank spot with no name under the title "network operations lead." But then she remembered: Travis, the new network operations lead, had just started, and in that instant she was able to map the call out in her mind. Now she was ready.

She picked up the phone and dialed the helpdesk. When someone answered, Roxy pretended to have a cold. Acting as Christy Salvador, Roxy told the person on the phone that she hoped they were training everyone correctly and that there had been a slight change in policy. She said she had a task that needed to be done ASAP. She said, "I don't need confirmation that it has been done. I just want you to do it." She asked that Travis be put on the phone and added, "This new guy better not mess this up." Travis, who no doubt had already heard about his demanding boss's reputation, rushed to the phone. Still posing as the director, Roxy told Travis that problems with data storage required them to delete all security logs, starting with the ASA Firewall, which she remembered from reading the firewall engineer job description online. Travis nervously did as he was told. He deleted all the logs, believing he was saving the company from a larger storage problem that may lead to loss of critical business data.

Roxy felt like she'd crossed the finish line. She thought for a minute and realized she may have to validate that they actually deleted the logs that traced her back to the network damage. For the moment, though, she felt good about what she had done and decided to show her face to her boss before she headed home. As Roxy poked her head out of the director's office to see if the coast was clear, she saw two guys carrying a computer. Roxy quickly stepped through the doorway and closed the door behind her. The two guys wore shirts emblazoned with the YNS Group logo and the words, "Computer Forensics Team." Before they opened their mouths to speak, Roxy told them the director just started a very important conference call and that she would probably be finished in an hour. The two men looked at each other, then at Roxy, and thanked her for the information.

As she started her way down the hall, Roxy looked into the room where the computer that brought down the company network was located. She immediately noticed it was gone. "Oh, no!" she thought, "That was the computer the forensics team just carried down the hall."

# Chapter 4

## A Voyage Too Deep

That night, Roxy thought about the computer and how the forensics team took it into their office. She knew she had to act quickly in order to thwart forensics from learning about her involvement. Since they picked up the computer just before close of business, they would be unlikely to analyze it that day. She felt she should go into work early, ahead of the forensic analysts, and get to it before they do. All she could think about was how she downloaded all of her electronic personnel files from the intranet onto that computer. She knew the files would turn up somewhere on that computer, whether among the temporary Internet files or on the desktop where she saved them before inserting the USB thumb drive.

The next morning, Roxy got dressed and headed to work at 6:00 a.m., hours ahead of most employees. As she walked into the building, she noticed the janitor who had given her access to the director's office was sitting in his car several rows away, looking at her. She thought he was probably wondering why she didn't park in the director's spot. Roxy walked closer to the building and didn't see a parking space for the director, so she just figured he was being nosey. "He's probably more interested in checking me out than the fact that I'm arriving so early," she thought.

She walked into the building and stopped in front of the directory sign. After she located the forensics team area, she realized it had badge-only access. She had not been cleared for this part of the fourth floor. Yet at this point, Roxy was determined to find a way in. On her way to the fourth floor she thought, "I was able to access the IT director's office and

17

get the network lead to delete network logs. I can do this, too."

As Roxy exited the elevator onto the fourth floor, she noticed the left side of the building was the badge-only access area. It had a badge scanner at the main door. The right side of the floor was an open office area for badge holders, but there were no scanners used to gain access. In the middle, there was a break area with tables and several vending machines.

Roxy headed straight for the vending machine area to avoid being questioned by anyone. She purchased a muffin and juice from one of the machines and sat at a table to eat. As she ate, she watched a few of the early risers go into and out of the badge-only area. A couple of the employees from the other area came over and sat a few tables away from her. She looked at their badges and noticed how simple they were; just a white background, company logo, and company name. She knew the badge wouldn't work without the necessary computer chip, but seeing the badges gave her an idea.

Roxy threw away what was left of her muffin and juice and headed to the elevator to go back to her temporary desk. She remembered exactly what the badge looked like and attempted to recreate it using the graphic design software installed on her computer. She couldn't make an exact match but, from a distance, the logo placement and wording looked nearly the same. She printed the fake badge and scoured the surrounding desks for a badge holder. She found a see-through holder, but it was a little wider than the badges used to access the fourth floor. Roxy felt it would do.

At nearly 7:30 a.m., thirty minutes before most of the employees normally arrived, Roxy decided to head back to the fourth floor with her fake badge. When she entered the floor this time, she realized there was a smoker's room next to the far end of the break area. She saw three people walking from the door to the badge-only access area to the smoker's room. Roxy decided to follow them in.

Roxy, a one-time smoker, asked the most talkative one in the bunch if he had a cigarette. He happily obliged. Instead of sitting away from the group to avoid being noticed, Roxy joined in on their conversation and started talking as if she had known them for years. She smiled a lot and added to their jokes, attempting to make them feel comfortable with her. As they all finished their cigarettes, Roxy put her barely smoked cigarette out and announced that she was trying to quit. The talkative man said he had given up that fight. Everyone laughed and made their way toward the badge-only access area.

Roxy purposely stayed in the back of the group, but made sure not to be the last person. When the first person scanned his badge on the scanner to unlock the door, he held the door open for the next person to walk through without having to scan. The person in front of Roxy turned and looked at her as he held open the door. Roxy flashed her fake badge, and he gave her a smile as he took a step back to let her walk in before him. She was able to walk right in without a key or a badge. While the badge system seemed intimidating from a distance, Roxy realized anyone who looked as if they belonged inside could easily make their way in, just as she was doing.

Once inside, Roxy immediately glanced around the area and saw a sign pointing out the forensics area. The three men headed one way while Roxy headed the other: to forensics. She entered the room and saw that there were nearly 30 computers on the floor. Papers with incident numbers and descriptions were taped to each one. She knew her time was running short, so she started reading the incident descriptions on each computer. When she had made her way through nearly half the computers, she noticed two computers sitting next to what appeared to be the main work area of the forensics lab. She stopped and headed toward them. She immediately saw the incident report for a computer virus that said, "high priority" and knew she had found the machine she inserted the USB thumb drive into the day of her interview.

Roxy did not want to take the entire computer with her, so she decided to remove the hard drive instead. She learned in college that all of a computer's data is stored in its drive. Roxy didn't want to leave it without a drive—that would be too obvious—so she took a spare drive out of one of the drawers in the forensics lab and replaced it with the drive she removed from the computer. Roxy took the drive that contained the data and quickly left the lab.

She headed out the main door back through the secure area. She was moving quickly toward the elevator and was about to step on but before she knew it nearly bumped into someone exiting to that floor. She looked up, and realized it was the janitor that let her into the director's office. "Excuse me," she said, as she tried to walk into the elevator. He shocked her by responding, "Good morning, Ms. Roxy!"

Roxy was stunned, as the janitor shouldn't have known her name, since she was posing as the IT director just the day prior. Remembering she had seen him in the parking lot earlier that morning, she concluded that the janitor had his own agenda, and he wanted to use Roxy for his benefit. He told her he had been watching her, and knew what she had been up to. He told Roxy to meet him for lunch at the barbeque grill at the end of the street. He told her to be there at noon if she wanted him to keep quiet about her activities.

Roxy silently slipped into the elevator, barely able to control her shaking. She wondered what this janitor knew about her and why he wanted to meet her. Her heart raced faster than it did when she first walked into the building for her interview. She was unsure whether she should entertain the janitor or just blow him off altogether. She quickly realized she couldn't ignore the situation. There was too much at stake. Roxy started thinking about her career and the possibility of prison time. She also thought about her negligence and how she might even lose her fiancé once he found out. These thoughts distracted Roxy all morning. Finally, at the last minute, Roxy decided to meet the janitor at the restaurant.

When Roxy arrived there, she didn't see the janitor anywhere. She started wondering if this was some sort of setup. She thought, "This can't be happening. I shouldn't have taken it this far." She decided to leave and go home to think everything through. As she got up from the table, she heard someone calling her name. She looked to the far corner of the restaurant, saw the janitor sitting alone, and joined him.

The janitor introduced himself as a friend that could make her rich – if she complied with his wishes. He told Roxy he had been watching her and knew what she was up to. He told her she had been able to access some areas in the building that even he couldn't access. He was not cleared to clean the badge-only area. Roxy asked, "What do you mean?" The janitor explained that he was working covertly for an overseas company. He was planted at the YNS Group as a janitor with orders to gather data about a new product the company was launching. Roxy quickly stood up and said, "There's no way I'll help you!" The janitor responded by telling Roxy she had to help him. If she didn't, he would turn her in – or something worse.

He asked her to have a seat once again, which she did, reluctantly. He went on to explain there were some influential people that would pay her a substantial amount of money to help him. He told her she didn't want to turn her back on this opportunity because she may face consequences she may not be able to recover from. Roxy had maintained a steely resolve until now, but finally her nerves began to get the best of her. She didn't know who this "janitor" worked for, or what he was capable of doing. She didn't want to find out what his veiled threat really meant, or the source of the money he referred to. Out of fear for her life and family, Roxy asked the janitor what he needed done.

The janitor told Roxy she was making a good decision and gave her a letter outlining specific instructions. She feared he wanted to use her for his corporate espionage so that all the fingerprints and evidence pointed to her. He told her he might need a few more things done when she finished the initial task, but that when she was done she would receive a check for $400,000 and would never see him again. At that point, it wasn't the money that motivated her, but the feeling that she was really in over her head. She needed all this to be over. She called her boss and told him an emergency had come up and that she would be back to work in the morning. She went home to unwind and look over the instructions.

# Chapter 5

# The Chain Letter

The instructions were short and to the point. The janitor and his employers wanted Roxy to send a CD containing a malicious PowerPoint file to as many YNS Group employees as possible, including the president and vice president of the company. The catch was that she had to make sure the employees and executives opened the file without her being caught. It was noted that the file, once opened, installed a keystroke logger onto every affected computer to track every key entered on every keyboard. These activities would be recorded via screenshots and e-mailed to the overseas competitor.

Roxy quickly realized it would be foolish to try to send the file from her own e-mail account. She thought long and hard about the best way to send the files to everyone. She decided once again to use Travis, the newly hired network operations lead. Roxy figured if she sent the file to him, she could gain access to his e-mail account and use that to send the files. Roxy opened the CD. She noticed there were three files: two PowerPoint and one text file named "readme."

The readme file provided instructions for configuring the malicious PowerPoint. It explained the exact steps to configure the software to produce e-mail screenshots for the overseas competitor. Roxy decided to configure the file to send her screenshots of Travis's computer activity, so that she could get his password. With that, she could access his email account and use it to blast out the malicious PowerPoint that would, in turn, send screenshots overseas. She created a free account online and added that e-mail address as the recipient to receive the screenshots and keystrokes. She figured this would also give her a chance to see how the program worked. She wanted to make sure that her method of attack would be effective before sending it to the president and vice-president of the YNS Group.

Roxy decided to rename the file before sending it to Travis, thus increasing the chance he would open it. She knew Travis was a new employee and that he was probably curious about making a bonus his first year; she even asked a related question in her interview. She quickly changed the PowerPoint that secretly installed the malicious software, editing it down into three slides. On those three pages she provided information about bonuses within the company. She then named the document "Getting a Bonus at YNS Group." Since she was using a bogus account not related to the company's e-mail, she thought she'd note in her e-mail signature that she was an intern sending the document to all new employees along with instructions to direct all questions to Human Resources. She figured Travis might think the intern just didn't know any better and look past it.

Roxy marked the message "urgent" and e-mailed it to Travis. Sure enough, not 15 minutes later, she began receiving e-mails from the program with screenshots of his activity. The first few e-mails contained only screenshots of her altered PowerPoint. Twenty minutes after that she received additional screenshots. These showed captured passwords used by Travis to log into different servers to administer the company network. She noticed that Travis also logged into several personal e-mail and shopping accounts with the same password he used to administer the company servers. She thought that since he was using the same password for his personal and business accounts, that his password to access the company e-mail was likely the same also.

Roxy decided to log into the company's online webmail page to see if the password worked. Sure enough, the password worked. Roxy couldn't believe that Travis used the same password for everything. Now that she had access to Travis's e-mail account, she decided to send the malicious PowerPoint file to the YNS Group executives and employees with the e-mail settings configured to send the data to the overseas competitor. She knew she needed everyone at the YNS Group to open the file, so she decided to send it in two separate e-mails. She remembered in her interview that the CTO mentioned an upcoming summit for YNS Group leaders. They planned to call the summit "Leaders: Be Leaders," or simply "LBL Summit."

For the e-mail to the YNS Group presidents, Roxy decided to include in her fake slides some phrases from the company website describing the summit. She named the document "LBL Summit Update." She created a new fake e-mail account and gave it the name of the venue where the summit was to be held. She wrote the message as if she was the venue host. In it, she asked if the information on the slides was correct and could she include it in the venue's monthly newsletter. Roxy sent the e-mail off to the YNS Group presidents.

At that point, Roxy was ready to send an e-mail to every YNS Group employee. This was easy to do since the company had a distribution list that included the e-mail addresses of all the employees. What was even better was that anyone could use it. At that point, Roxy had to maximize the number of people that would open the message. She remembered an e-mail she received in college that was supposed to be an electronic petition but was actually a student experiment. Instead of a petition, Roxy decided to create a fake Amber Alert about a missing child to send to all YNS Group employees. She searched Google for images of a young girl and copied them into PowerPoint. She wrote a few sentences about helping the family by looking at the pictures on the PowerPoint and sending the e-mail to everyone they knew. She felt that once an employee got the e-mail, he or she would likely forward it to fellow employees and possibly others outside the company as well, thereby increasing the chances the message would get opened. Roxy then sent the e-mail to all of the YNS Group employees.

Roxy thought, "My job here is done." The janitor had previously instructed her to meet him at the same place in 24 hours, so she headed back to the barbeque grill to wait for him. When the janitor arrived, Roxy told him she had completed her required tasks. "Now that I'm done I want my money," she said. The janitor looked at her and laughed. He told her she was in no position to negotiate. Then he told her that although she was able to get Travis to delete the logs on the day she called, she had not thought to ask about the backup tapes. The janitor told her all logs were archived on tape at the end of each day. He said he removed the logs from Tuesday, but Monday's logs were already archived to backup. He told her he slipped someone in data storage a few hundred dollars in exchange for those logs, and would keep them close. This was his insurance policy that she would do as she was told.

The janitor told her she had done well and that his boss just sent him a message saying that he was receiving data from employees throughout the company. However, he had another task he needed her to perform. The janitor told her the company president would be going out of town for a business trip the following day. He told her he would meet her at the airport. He needed her to help him get the president's laptop. He said this would be her last task and that she would be rewarded when she was finished.

# Chapter 6

## The Day She Will Never Forget

Roxy woke up Saturday morning and decided she had to tell her fiancé everything that had happened. She knew he would be disappointed in her, but it felt like everything happened so fast. The time had come to let him know. Roxy went to her fiancé, who was asleep in bed, and shook him a few times. As he woke, she told him they needed to talk. Her fiancé quickly sat up and asked what was wrong.

Roxy told him everything. He was shocked that she had gotten herself into this predicament. He said, "This ends now. You have to report this to your boss and the police as soon as possible." Roxy told him she couldn't, that the janitor—whoever he really was—had threatened her. She told him she was going to end it that day, but that she had to go to the airport first. He looked at her in disbelief, and shook his head as Roxy walked away.

Roxy was a wreck when she arrived at the airport. She was normally a confident woman, rarely at a loss for words. That day, however, trying to figure out how she got into this mess made her sick to her stomach. She was always witty, but had never used her wit for crime. As she paced the airport, a stranger approached her.

He wore a business suit and was clean-shaven. He said, "Hi, Roxy. I'm an associate of your friend, the janitor. I'll be accompanying you through the security checkpoint to help you secure the item."

"You mean the laptop?" Roxy replied.

"Yes!" the man said. He gave her a plane ticket, told her she would need it to get through security, but that she wouldn't take a flight. He told her they would both get in line in front of the president. He would stand between them and as they sent their items through the scanner, he would hold up the line while she snatched the laptop at the end of the conveyer belt. He told her she would have about 15 seconds to get the laptop and make her way to the other side in the direction of the security entrance.

Roxy took the ticket and asked where the janitor was. The man said he would meet up with them afterwards. He told her to go get something to eat and wait for him to signal her into the line. After about an hour, Roxy saw the YNS Group president. She recognized him from many of the company newsletters and marketing materials.

Just as she saw the president, the janitor's associate waved his arm for her to join him in line. He was right in front of the president. When she walked up to him he said, "I hope the ladies room wasn't too dirty this time," and winked at Roxy. She was extremely nervous. She and the janitor's associate stood in silence as they made their way toward security.

According to plan, the president's personal items entered the conveyer belt at the same time as their shoes, keys, and belts. The janitor's associate started holding up the line by setting off the metal detectors with items in his pocket. At the same time, Roxy made her way past security. She quickly grabbed the laptop and placed it next to her feet as she rushed to put her shoes on. Once both shoes were on, she grabbed the laptop and started to stand up to make her exit. As she stood, she felt firm pressure on her shoulder. She turned around to find a large man wearing a suit pulling her back by her shoulder while three police officers approached. In her peripheral, she saw the janitor's associate heading toward the exit. Roxy needed no time to realize her brief life as a criminal was coming to an end.

Roxy was taken to a small room in the airport. She had been sitting, alone, for about 10 minutes before the guy who grabbed her by the shoulder walked in. He identified himself as an airport security officer and asked her where she was going. Instead of answering, Roxy sat quietly. He told her she could call a lawyer, but things would go much smoother if she simply cooperated. Roxy, not wanting this to go any future, consented and told him everything. After listening to her tale, the officer, looking at Roxy with raised eyebrows, told her he would be back.

After waiting more than 30 minutes, Roxy became impatient and thought she should probably contact her fiancé to get a lawyer. Just as she stood up, the door swung open and the CTO of the YNS Group walked in with the airport security officer.

The officer told Roxy he pulled her into the office because she was acting extremely suspicious, and his security staff had noticed her behavior. She spent 30 minutes in the airport restaurant without eating or drinking anything. The entire time she was there, she ignored the wait staff and kept looking around. When she finally left the restaurant, she left her purse behind. He told her she exhibited all the signs of someone looking to perform an act of terror; leaving her purse behind clinched it for them. The security officer explained that he called the CTO after she told him her story. He asked her to retell the CTO everything.

Feeling ashamed, scared, and embarrassed, Roxy told the CTO everything she had been doing for the past few days, down to the last detail. When she finished the story, the CTO looked at Roxy, grinned, and started shaking his head. "Roxy," he said, "the good news is you're not going to jail." He told her the USB thumb drive she found on the day of her interview was part of a security awareness exercise. Just as he finished his sentence, the door opened. To Roxy's surprise, the janitor walked in.

The CTO told Roxy, "Meet Fred Thompson, YNS Group's network security lead." Roxy's jaw dropped.

She said, "But, but how?"

The CTO explained that the network problems that occurred when she used the USB thumb drive were mere coincidence. He said their security team—which made up the We Own You virus—was testing the security shrewdness of its employees by planting USB thumb drives in areas outside the building. He said the drive was configured to take screenshots and send them to security, so they knew exactly who used it. Because of the network problems, the security team had not checked the screenshots until the next day, which is when they started watching Roxy.

Fred interrupted to tell Roxy they started watching her with the security cameras. They couldn't figure out what she was doing or why she kept prowling the hallways. He explained that one of the janitors became ill on Tuesday. As Fred was putting the janitor's cleaning cart away for him, he saw Roxy trying to get into the IT director's office. He had seen the director leave, and since he knew Roxy was up to something, he decided he would test her. Fred said he was surprised when she told him that was her office, but he figured he'd see how far she would go.

"That is when he came to me," said the CTO. "We have had a hard time persuading the president to fund a security awareness campaign, so we decided to use this as an opportunity to prove a point. We didn't want you to take this too far, so we decided to join in but control the outcome. Taking the president's laptop was the last task. We were going to sit you down to talk about it on Monday."

The CTO told Roxy he didn't want to fire her. While she had made some bad choices, they had put her in a position to make them, and they were representative of the poor security decisions that employees make all the time. He said, "We'd like you to join the security team. Not only did you demonstrate that you have a surprising amount of knowledge about computer security, but you now also have first-hand knowledge of why corporate security awareness is so important. We'd like you to start by writing a full report outlining what happened and how you took advantage of our staff. You will be in charge of leading our security awareness campaign, telling your story to employees, and helping them to understand that this could happen to them. Although what happened to you was ultimately just an exercise, a similar situation could happen to any employee, with a real spy as the janitor, new-hire, or even a seasoned employee. We don't want anyone else falling for fake badges, fake e-mail, imposter directors, or imposter smokers; we want to keep our employees safe and out of prison."

*Note: This story was fictitious — intended only to provoke thought about events that could occur. In the real world, I would never promote an employee who exhibited Roxy's behavior, or applaud the actions of the security staff. Continue reading for the story's lessons learned and tips for preventing real world attacks.*

# Part 2

## *The Lessons*

# #1

## Watch Out For Social Engineers

When people hear the term "social engineering," they likely think it is some kind of profession or high-level graduate program. Social engineering is far from a reputable academic program, though. It involves the manipulation or deception of someone for the purposes of fraud, monetary gain, or, in rare cases, fun. A social engineer takes advantage of human emotions such as fear, trust, or the desire to help others.

Roxy used Travis' anxiety about being a new employee and wanting to make an impression on a demanding IT director. She was able to get Travis, who didn't think logically about what he did, to delete important network logs. He actually felt relieved about what he had done because he wanted to help the company with a larger storage issue, at least that's what Roxy led him to believe. Both his fear and his desire to help pushed him to take action. If the janitor wasn't really the network security lead, someone with the master key seeing a disappointed director might have opened that door without first verifying her identity. Moreover, the smokers with badge-only access to the secure area built trust with Roxy in just a short time. They were fascinated by her looks, but she also smoked and laughed with them, which caused them to drop their guard.

Here are some tips to avoid social engineering:

• Always verify the name of the person you are talking to when someone calls and you don't recognize the voice. You can use small talk, but ask direct questions only the real person would know.

•Never allow someone into a badge-only area without swiping his or her badge and gaining authorization from the badge scanner. Even if they appear to have the right badge and seem like a nice person, they should still swipe.

• Be careful of vendors, contractors, and disgruntled employees who ask questions about business matters that should be of no concern to them.

• Be wary of suspicious e-mail and always think twice before opening attachments, even those sent by seemingly valid sources.

Some indicators or warning signs of social engineering:

• Someone claiming to be an authority figure.

• A caller who does not want to provide a return phone number.

• Unnecessary compliments or words of admiration.

• Someone claiming they need something urgently that simply can't wait.

• Someone exhibiting any of the above behaviors who avoids your questions.

# #2

# Be mindful of Open Source Information

Open source information, otherwise known as open source intelligence, is any information obtained through public sources. These sources can be personal blogs, websites, and search engines such as Google, Yahoo!, and MSN. Along with OSI, some attackers look in less obvious places for information, including dumpsters. These "dumpster divers" will look for any form of intellectual property that may not have made it to the company shredder.

Here are some tips to minimize the impacts of open source intelligence and dumpster diving:

• Treat all information posted online as if it will be accessible to the world forever.

• Never post information online that is sensitive to yourself or the company.

• When in doubt, shred it! It is better to shred everything than to unknowingly toss out intellectual property.

• Be careful about what you post to social networking sites, even professional ones. An attacker may be able to piece your entire life story together, or learn confidential business details, by aggregating portions of information from different websites.

• If you are in charge of posting job announcements, use only general information about the business and its systems. Specific details can alert attackers to potential vulnerabilities.

# #3

## Be careful opening E-mail

E-mail is a great mode of communication, and is often the first choice for businesses to reach their employees. Because it is so widely used, attackers use e-mail to target specific people or organizations. As in the case with Roxy, the janitor gave her a CD to send malicious software (malware) to the presidents and employees of the YNS Group. When coupled with other attack mechanisms, including social engineering, attackers have an increased chance of successfully installing their malware on an individual's computer.

Roxy understood that most people are aware of spam. She knew people tend to delete messages they feel nervous about. Because she was charged with the task of making as many people open her e-mail message as possible, she had to tap into one of the human emotions to increase her chances. She played into the YNS Group executives' trust by using the name of the upcoming Leadership Summit and a fake e-mail account from the summit venue. When she sent the fake Amber Alert in the form of a chain letter, she knew the YNS Group employees' desire to want to help would cause them to open the PowerPoint—at least to see the pictures.

Another form of e-mail to be cautious about is called phishing. Phishing is a form of social engineering used to steal someone's identity. Phishing attacks are often used for monetary gain and rely on compromising the victim's financial credentials. To effectively initiate a phishing attack, the attacker normally needs the victim to click a link or access a website. Many times, e-mail messages are sent as a broadcast to multiple users. Common claims used in these messages include, "You must log in to verify your account before it is closed," or "Your account was fraudulently accessed." They specifically prey on human fear, which overshadows warning signs, such as not using the e-mail recipient's name in the message.

Here are some tips to help avoid e-mail attacks:

• Always verify that the sender is who he or she claims to be. Call them and ask if they sent the message.

• Avoid suspicious e-mails requesting personal information, even if everything else about the e-mail appears to be legitimate.

• Report any e-mails requesting usernames and/or passwords.

• Always encrypt e-mail (if your company offers it) and be wary of e-mail that isn't digitally signed.

• Avoid putting any personal or company information into an e-mail.

• Always report phishing or suspicious e-mails to your security department.

# #4

## Always report suspicious devices

Cyber Within begins with Roxy finding a USB thumb drive on the front steps of the YNS Group building. Anyone can easily find a similar drive lying around a parking lot or anywhere else and pick it up. That person may think they just scored by finding a drive, but would be sad to find out it installed a keylogger onto their computer and sent screenshots to some unknown person. A keylogger logs keystrokes and is frequently used with most forms of malware. You should be as cautious about finding USB drives as you are about buying them.

Some popular auction sites have sellers listing USB thumb drives for very reasonable prices. If a price sounds too good to be true, it probably is. An attacker can load hidden malware into a drive and practically give it away to unsuspecting victims. Also, after purchasing a new thumb drive, it's best to wipe it clean with a cleaning utility before using it. Show caution when doing this, too, as some forms of malware may escape before you start the erasing process.

Here are some tips to help avoid being victimized by USB devices:

• Never use an unknown USB thumb drive on your company or home network.

• Be wary about where you purchase drives; check the reputation of the seller.

• Only use authorized devices on your company network. Your personal drive may contain some form of malware that you are unaware of. To prevent legal consequences, or the loss of your job, only use drives that have been authorized by your company.

• Always erase new drives clean before using them.

# #5

## Always report malware or abnormal computer behavior

When her screen locked up and Roxy couldn't move her mouse, she knew the USB thumb drive did something to her computer. In such cases, the best thing to do is contact the service desk. At the very least, they should conduct an investigation to determine whether your computer does indeed contain malware, or may simply need to be fixed or replaced. It is best to know the types of behavior most malware exhibit.

Depending upon how the malware was programmed, it may perform a variety of actions. Some malware will start every time a certain program is started. Other types work silently in the background. In either case, the operating system will sometimes respond by displaying error messages, or by simply not starting other programs.

Here are some tips to help you recognize malware:

- Your computer is running slower than usual.

- Your Internet home page keeps changing.

- You keep getting security warning pop-ups*.

- Your CPU usage is higher than normal.

- Working applications start crashing.

- You notice odd error messages.

*See **BONUS TIPS** in "Employee Quick Tips" section.

# #6

## Protect your passwords

Travis used the same password on all his personal and business e-mail accounts. When one password was compromised, Roxy had the keys to his kingdom. Using the same password for all accounts is bad practice. Although it may be much easier to remember the same password, if an attacker hacks one account they will have access to all accounts. The best type of password to use is a passphrase.

Passphrases are both easy to remember and hard to crack. An example of a simple passphrase is 1L0v3Cyb3rW1ithin. The first two "l"s were replaced with the number 1, the "o" was replaced with a zero, and the "e"s were replaced with the number 3. Remembering numerous characters that are mixed with meaningless numbers can be a daunting challenge—especially if you have to use different variances for each account. However, creating passphrases that have some meaning to you makes it much easier. Plus, using a passphrase is much more secure than using your birth date or street address.

Here are some tips for creating better passwords:

- Always use passphrases.
- Never write down your password.
- Never share your password with anyone for any reason.
- Never make your password reset questions too easy.

• Do not use the same password on all your accounts.

# #7

## Look out for employees exhibiting suspicious behavior

Roxy displayed some very suspicious behavior that raised eyebrows in the airport, but not at her new job. No one reported her prowling around the office, peeking around corners, and spending excessive time in break areas. On the other hand, security staff at the airport noticed her behavior right away. Sure, one could argue that it is the job of the security staff to maintain awareness at the airport. While I do agree, I also believe employees should stay conscious of their surroundings. This is to protect themselves and others. For example, employees who have become suicidal or "gone postal" often exhibit suspicious behavior and warning signs before attempting to harm themselves or others.

Here are some common suspicious behaviors to watch out for:

- An employee avoids contact when approached.

- An employee spends excessive time in break areas.

- An employee is caught looking over one's shoulder while on the computer. This is known as "shoulder surfing."

- An employee suddenly acts nervous.

# Reporting Incidents

If you make a mistake, tell someone! Even if you give out a password, forward along an e-mail, or give someone access to a secured area and later feel funny about it – report it!

Write down your security department's contact information, and keep this sheet handy in the case that you need to report an incident. Fill out your office and system information in pencil, as it may change from time to time.

**Reporting in my organization:**

Incident reporting hotline: _____

E-mail hotline: _____

**Information they may need:**

Confidential information affected?  Y or N

Building: _____

Floor and department: _____

**Affected system:**

Computer name: _____

IP addresses: _____

Computer hardware: _____

Operating system and version: _____

# Employee Quick Tips

**1. Tips to avoid social engineering:**

- Verify caller identity by using small talk and direct questions.
- Never allow anyone into a badge-only area without first swiping his or her badge.
- Be careful of vendors, contractors, or disgruntled employees asking odd questions about business matters.
- Be wary of e-mail messages that seem suspicious.
- Always think twice before opening e-mail attachments.

**2. Tips to notice social engineering:**

- Someone claiming to be someone with authority.
- A caller refusing to provide a return phone number.
- The giving of unnecessary compliments or words of admiration.
- Someone claiming they need something urgently, something that simply cannot wait.
- Someone exhibiting the behaviors above who also avoids being questioned.

**3. Tips to minimize the impacts of open source intelligence and dumpster diving:**

- Treat all information posted online as if it will be available to everyone forever.
- Never post information online that is sensitive to yourself or the company.
- When in doubt, shred it! Do not toss out anything that may be construed as intellectual property.
- Be careful about what you post to social networking sites. Bits of information from all over the Web can be aggregated to create a clear picture of your life and habits.

# Employee Quick Tips

**4. Tips to help avoid e-mail attacks:**

• Always verify that the sender is who he or she claims to be.

• Report any e-mails that request usernames, passwords, or personal information.

• If possible, always encrypt or digitally sign e-mail.

• Avoid putting personal or company information into an e-mail.

• Always report phishing or suspicious e-mails to your security department.

**5. Tips to help avoid becoming victimized to USB devices:**

• Never use an unknown USB drive on your company or home network.

• Be wary about where you purchase drives; always check the seller's reputation (and their distributors).

• Only use authorized devices on your company network. Your personal drive may contain some form of malware that you are unaware of. To prevent legal consequences or the loss of your job, only use company authorized drives.

• Always erase new drives clean before using them.

**6. Tips to help recognize malware:**

• Your computer is running slower than usual.

• Your Internet home page keeps changing.

• You keep getting security warning pop-ups.

• Your CPU usage is higher than normal.

• Working applications start crashing.

• You notice odd error messages.

# Employee Quick Tips

**7. Tips for creating better passwords:**

- Always use passphrases.
- Never write your password down.
- Never give your password to anyone, for any reason.
- Never make your password reset questions too easy.
- Do not use the same password on all accounts.

**8. Tips to recognize suspicious behaviors:**

- An employee avoids contact when approached.
- An employee spends excessive time in break areas.
- An employee is caught "shoulder surfing."
- An employee suddenly acts nervous.

**BONUS TIPS:**

- Exercise caution before clicking abbreviated URLs (those condensed by URL shortening services, hiding their true destination).
- Exercise caution when accessing websites that host third-party content (such as applications on Facebook and other social networking sites).
- Be wary of security and warning alerts, no matter how legitimate they appear. Always report suspicious antivirus software activity!
- Bottom line: use caution when browsing the Web! Thousands of legitimate websites are compromised daily, and one click can install data-stealing malware without notice.

*Provided courtesy of CyberWithin.com*

# Awareness Resources

For more information on social engineering and other cyber threats visit:

**Anti-Phishing Working Group**

Provides news on phishing trends, tips, and advice if you happen to give your personal information out.

http://www.antiphishing.org/


**California State Polytechnic University, Pomona**

Provides phishing examples, signs of phishing, and tips to avoid being "hooked."

http://www.csupomona.edu/~ehelp/security/security_phishing.html


**Microsoft Online Safety**

Provides fraud prevention tips and advice on passwords, e-mail, spam, and also shopping.

http://www.microsoft.com/protect/fraud/


**OnGuardOnline**

Provides tips and advice on social networking sites, malware, e-mail scams, P2P security, and more.

http://www.onguardonline.gov/default.aspx


**Stay Safe Online**

Provides a host of security resources for home users, small and medium size businesses, and primary and secondary education.

http://www.staysafeonline.org/

# Glossary

**Central Processing Unit (CPU):** the brain of a computer system that carries out instructions.

**Digital signature:** an electronic signature used to verify the authenticity of the sender.

**Dumpster diving:** a technique used to pilfer useful information that was thrown away in the trash.

**Encryption:** the process of converting plain text into a format not easily readable to unauthorized people.

**Firewall:** a network or system device used to block unauthorized connections.

**Forensics:** the application of science to identify evidence on computer systems.

**Hack:** to modify hardware or software for purposes other than its original design.

**Incident:** a distinct occurrence outside of the norm.

**Information Technology (IT):** the development of computer systems and their integration into business processes.

**Keylogger** (see keystroke logger)

**Keystroke logger:** software, or a hardware device, used to capture keyboard activity. Software keystroke loggers are often configured to send captures to the attacker.

**Logs:** data stored on a system that keeps track of system activities.

**Malicious software:** software created for malicious purposes. Often used to take over a computer, steal information, or stop services.

**Malware** (see malicious software)

**Network security:** processes and techniques used to secure a computer network.

**Open Source Information:** information obtained from public sources (e.g. the Internet, newspapers, magazines, etc.)

**Passphrase:** a stronger form of a password that is more memorable than mixing random characters.

**Phishing:** a form a fraud. Phishing relies on legitimate looking e-mail to entice users to give up sensitive information, or even to download malware.

**Scanner:** an electronic device used to read a digital image.

**Shoulder surfing:** the act of looking over someone's shoulder in order to see unauthorized information without being caught.

**Social engineering:** the art of manipulating or deceiving someone to disclose information.

**URL:** uniform resource locator, or otherwise called Web address.

**USB:** universal serial bus used to link a computer and peripheral device.

**Virus:** a common term used to describe various forms of malicious software.

**Vulnerability:** a weakness in a system that can be used to take over a computer system.

# Thank You

Thank you for buying and reading this book. If you find this information helpful to others, or beneficial to safeguarding corporate secrets and preventing identity theft, you can help!

As an independent author, there's no huge marketing budget or team of publicists available...but that's okay. If you don't mind offering a few minutes of your time—writing a review on Amazon.com, mentioning this book on your blog, Tweeting about it on Twitter, or telling your friends about it on Facebook—you'd be doing me a huge service while helping to educate others! Surprisingly, these little things make a big difference!

If you have any questions or specific comments, please feel free to e-mail me: marcos@cyberwithin.com

Best wishes,
Marcos Christodonte II

# Quick Order Form

**E-mail orders:** orders@proactiveassurance.com *(send this form)*

**Phone orders:** Call 800-615-5169

**Fax orders:** 800-615-5169 *(send this form)*

**Please send more information on:**

☐ Consulting    ☐ Speaking/Seminars    ☐ Mailing List

**Name:** _____

**Address:** _____

**City:** _____ **State:** _____ **Zip:** _____

**Telephone:** _____

**E-mail address:** _____

**Bulk discounts available:**

For bulk discounts, send an e-mail to: orders@proactiveassurance.com

**www.CyberWithin.com**

CPSIA information can be obtained
at www.ICGtesting.com
Printed in the USA
LVHW042332090119
603402LV00009B/253